AT HOME IN THE WOODS

Written by Pamela Guselle
Illustrated by Valerie Bouthyette

Published by Skopelos Press
Toronto, ON
www.skopelospress.com

ISBN 978-0-9877786-6-6

For Pascal, my husband, friend and partner.
Special thanks to PJG and JFT.

Deep in the woods, a big, burly bear
Lumbers out
Of his cozy lair,
Foraging for food,
At home in the woods.

Sunrise....a brand-new day;
Fawns run and leap
As they come out to play.
Clearings are playgrounds
At home in the woods.

They soften the nest with leaf litter and twigs.
Parents work hard
As each of them digs,
Awaiting their newborn
At home in the woods.

In tucked away corners, under moss-covered rocks,
Hidden between
Lilies and phlox,
Small ones find comfort
At home in the woods.

The woodpecker uses his beak like a hammer.
Looking for insects,
He makes quite a clamour.
Tap, tap, tap, tap,
At home in the woods.

In a soft fungus garden, on an old, fallen log
Between mushrooms and toadstools
And next to a bog,
The tiniest creatures find shelter
At home in the woods.

Through burrow-like tunnels, they shimmy and slide,
Deep underground,
They live, feed, and hide.
Rarely seen, rarely heard, but
At home in the woods.

Otters hunt dinner of mussels and fish;
They splash in streams
And dive with a swish.
They feed, and they frolic
At home in the woods.

Dewdrops shine like crystal beads
Upon a web
Among the weeds.
Spiders sit and wait to eat
At home in the woods.

Basking and bathing, they lounge and laze,
Enjoying the sun's
Warm, dappled rays.
Happy and content
At home in the woods.

Up pops a chipmunk with little brown ears;
A twitch of a whisker,
He then disappears.
Cheeks full of seed,
At home in the woods.

The whispering wind and cool, shadowed breeze
Float through the air
And rustle the trees.
Ears are attuned
At home in the woods.

Beavers gnaw; the tree falls with a thud.
They build their lodges
With branches and mud.
Snug in their den
At home in the woods.

The rain's pelting down, thunderbolts crash,
And the sky becomes bright
With each lightning flash.
They'll outwait the scare; warm and dry,
At home in the woods.

With little masked faces and bushy tails,
They swim and prowl
Near the forest trail,
Eating crayfish and frogs
At home in the woods.

Tracks at the edge of a pond so still
Mark those who came
To drink their fill.
Whose tracks are these?
At home in the woods.

Shhh....what's that sound?
A wolf's howl in the wind.
Stay close to the ground!
Take cover from danger
At home in the woods.

High in the trees, birds rest their wings
In nests they have built.
They flutter, clasp, cling.
Feeling safe and secure
At home in the woods.

Coyotes come back from the evening hunt.
They greet one another,
The leader in front.
A "Yip" means "Hello"
At home in the woods.

From towering treetops to the tiniest brook,
Between branches and boulders,
Wherever you look,
The wonders of wildlife are....
At home in the woods.

Made in the USA
Columbia, SC
22 October 2021

47346010R00027